THE
DIFFERENCE
GOD
MAKES

*Living as if
God Matters*

THE
DIFFERENCE
GOD
MAKES

*Living as if
God Matters*

World Wide Publications
1303 Hennepin Avenue
Minneapolis, MN 55403

8016BOOKCOVR
129

World Wide Publications is the book publishing division of the
Billy Graham Evangelistic Association.

The Difference God Makes by Peter Haile was originally
published by Inter Varsity Press.

All Scripture quotations unless otherwise indicated are from the
Revised Standard Version of the Bible copyrighted 1946, 1952,
1971, 1973.

ISBN   0-89066-101-4

Printed in the United States of America

Fifth Printing 1987

World Wide Publications
1303 Hennepin Avenue
Minneapolis, MN 55403

Acknowledgments

Many people have had a part in bringing this book to birth.

I want to thank students and colleagues at The Stony Brook School who have listened over the years to my attempts to explain God's truth in chapel and in classes.

I want to thank Inter-Varsity staff members and students at Cedar Campus who in the summer of 1979 likewise were subjected to much of the material here.

I am also grateful to my daughter-in-law, Susan, for her work in typing the manuscript.

Introduction:
Scotch Tape and Kleenex

When my daughter was three, she was often told that writing on the walls of our house with pencil, crayon, lipstick or magic marker was to be avoided on pain of serious consequences. She was assured that heavy-handed justice would pursue her if she indulged in this admittedly entertaining activity.

One day, however, the urge to leave her mark on the world got the better of her. Let me say in her favor that she did not go berserk, as some children do, and cover the whole wall. In fact, she was extraordinarily restrained—the mark was not more than, say, an eighth of an inch long. But there it was, in red.

Remorse struck after a period of unknown length. As I was quietly working at my desk, she came in and asked for my Scotch tape. Normally I insist on knowing what my Scotch tape is going to be used for. But this time she seemed to be saying so loudly that her purpose was confidential and none of my business that I let it go with one stipulation, that it be returned as soon as she was finished.

Later, I happened to go into her room and was surprised to see a piece of Kleenex carefully Scotch-taped to the wall. I investigated further. Underneath, I found the eighth-of-an-inch red mark, elaborately hidden.

She was trying to cover up what she had done. It's a common occupation, and the older we get, the more skillful we become at it. Instead of Scotch tape and Kleenex, we use borrowed words and manufactured attitudes. We try to obscure what we are and what we have done by putting up a front, pretending to be something that we are not.

There's a way out of this covering-up business, and it is by seeing what God has done for us—the difference that he really makes when he comes into our lives. When we see clearly who God really is and what he has done in saving us, we can finally begin to be ourselves. We can emerge from the shadows, throw away our fig leaves, meet God face to face and enjoy his companionship forever.

The purpose of this book is to look again at the character of God and trace the implications in our daily lives of who he is and what he's done.

Chapter one deals with the key to it all: faith. What does it really mean to believe in God? Is it a feeling or an act of the will?

Chapter two discusses the love of God—something we talk much about but often don't really understand or believe in.

In chapter three we trace the extent of God's self-giving. We see that what he has really done is to share his very life with us to the extent of making us one with him.

Chapter four searches out the implication of Christ's lordship, and chapter five affirms the fact that he is the great Initiator and Completer. It tackles the question of how much I am supposed to do and how much is God's responsibility.

In chapter six we look at God's commitment to be our Guide through life and ask whether this means that he will tell us whom to marry and what profession to choose. We discuss how we can distinguish between God's voice and our own feelings.

Chapters seven and eight deal with Jesus' great claims to be the Resurrection and the Life and the Bread of heaven. These stirring but strangely elusive statements need to take on meaning in our lives.

Finally, we examine the nature and meaning of "the kingdom of God" and the difference the coming of that kingdom makes. It is the difference God makes in our lives.

Battle
for Belief

1

Some while ago I was talking to a friend who was feeling out of touch with God and consequently upset, disturbed and edgy. And he was doing what most of us do in that situation: he was grubbing around inside trying to find out what he had done wrong. In fact, he was being quite belligerent about it. He was aggressively reconnoitering all the possible areas of enemy infiltration: defects in his devotional life, defects in his self-discipline, defects in his repentance from sin. His search for the enemy was thorough and intense. 'Round and 'round he went, trying to find out what he had done wrong. Fortunately, he hadn't yet got around to blaming everybody else for the problem. But when none of his searching unearthed the enemy or

brought victory any closer, he said plaintively,
"But aren't believers promised joy and peace?"

I stopped him and said, "Yes. *Believers* are
promised joy and peace." At that moment he saw
the point. He had been in pursuit of the wrong enemy. He'd been squandering his energy on fruitless
introspection instead of fighting the battle for belief. What had robbed him of his joy and peace and
had brought a sense of alienation from God was not
anything that he had done: it was what he had not
done. It was his failure to take God at his Word, to
act on the assumption that God really means what
he says—that was the trouble. Unbelief like this is
our most besetting sin, the sin that we are more
frequently guilty of than any other.

Unbelief is just as much of a sin as telling a lie,
being a hypocrite, cheating, losing your temper,
lusting after your neighbor's spouse—and far more
critical. At every point or moment in life we are
either acting in faith or outside of faith, and that is
what makes all the difference.

What is Faith?

Some people use the word faith to mean "self-con-
fidence, optimism, having good expectations about
the future." That's a legitimate use of the word, but
it is not what the Bible is talking about.

Some of us think of faith as intellectual assent to
right doctrines and feel that belief is having our
minds settled on the fact that the Bible is authorita-
tive, that Jesus was and is God, that Jesus' death
atones for our sins, and so on. But, important as
intellectual assent to certain doctrines is, it is only a
fractional part of true faith.

Others among us—and I suspect this constitutes the biggest group—think that faith is a means to an end. We look back to the day we were saved, and we remember that we came to a recognition that God is real and that we were in a wrong relationship to him and that this had to be put right. We responded to a call to confess our sins, and we claimed some promise like John 3:16 or 1 John 1:9. We had the wonderful feeling of being clean and new—indeed we were. We had come to Christ; we were new Christians, and it had all happened because we had believed, because we had exercised faith. So we identify belief with experiences like that.

Then again, we may look back to a crisis experience in our lives, such as when we had desperate physical or financial needs. I look back again and again to an occasion when I was working for Inter-Varsity Christian Fellowship in New England, and we had not been paid for three months. Our resources were down to just two or three dollars, left in our checking account to keep it open. My wife and I read Matthew 6:25-33 together, and we went down to our mailbox and found fifteen dollars in an envelope with our name on it.

On another occasion when we were equally desperate we again claimed the promise that "if God so clothes the grass of the field, which today is alive and tomorrow is thrown into the oven, will he not much more clothe you?" (Mt. 6:30). I drove up to a gas station to fill up, and as I opened the door of my car I found a ten-dollar bill sticking up out of the snow right under my eyes. The garage attendant said, "You may as well keep it; I don't know who dropped it." Personally, I suspect an angel put it there. But the point is that our needs were met. We were trusting God, believing in him, exercising faith. So we tend to identify faith with crisis experiences like that.

But faith is more than optimism; it's more than intellectual assent; it's more than an occasional resource to be used in emergencies.

Letting God be God

Faith is acting on the assumption that God is as good as his Word. By *his Word* I do not mean just a promise or a series of promises that he has made to us (though these are included); I mean the total revelation he has given us in Scripture and in history concerning who he is and what he has done. Scripture presents him to us above all as a Being, a Person, Someone who is. It does not present him to us as a series of propositions or even a series of promises. It reveals him to us as a Promiser.

The Bible's revelation of who God is, however, falls prey to the same tendency which affects all our relationships. We want to force people into the mold that we have designed for them. We build up an image of what we want our husband or wife, brother or sister or friend to be, and subconsciously we try to force them into that image. We do exactly the same thing with God. We try to force him into our own image, and so often that means that we start thinking of him—or at least dealing with him—on the basis of his being an impersonal dispenser of health, wealth and favorable circumstances. We view him as a divine vending machine; we put in our money and get out a candy bar of forgiveness, guidance or healing. Now, don't get me wrong. I believe that God forgives and guides and heals. *But the far greater truth is that he is the Forgiver, the Guide and the Healer.* He wants us to live our lives against the background of the greater truth, not the lesser one. He wants us to act moment by moment on the basis of his being and his character, revealed to us in his Word by his Spirit. That is faith. That is the Christian way of life.

Let me illustrate. God wants you and me to act moment by moment on the assumption that he is the great Forgiver. Yet I find many Christians laboring under a sense of guilt, struggling with feelings of being under the displeasure and judgment of God, cut off from him because of some sin that they cannot erase from their conscience or emotions. Back they go, mourning over that sin again, confessing it again, excusing themselves for it, enlarging it, and shadowboxing with it until they are utterly exhausted. All the time God has forgiven and forgotten it because he is the great Forgiver.

These unfortunate people have been fighting the wrong battle and have been on the track of the wrong enemy. Their real problem at the moment of their feeling guilty was not the sin they were thinking about but the one they ignored; namely, the sin of their own lack of faith in God and what he has proclaimed himself to be. God wanted them to believe in him as the Forgiver, and then he would have given them the freedom from their feelings of guilt. If they had looked to the character of God, they would have found rest.

But such belief is not easy. It involves letting go of the things of sight and sense: the sin, our aware-

ness of it, even our repentance over it, and transfer-
ring our attention, the gaze of our heart, to the un-
seen reality of the character of God revealed to us
in his Word and illumined to us by his Spirit.

Suppose that, in a moment of anger and frustration, I say something unkind to a friend. Immediately afterward—or, at least, as soon as my feeble
efforts at self-justification have subsided—I am
filled with remorse. I go to my friend and say how
sorry I am and ask her to forgive me. She then
says, "Forget it!" Now, faith is accepting my
friend's statement and acting on the assumption that
the angry words have been forgiven and the relationship restored. But let me ask you this: Is that
what you always do? Have you ever found yourself
going back to your friend and elaborating on your
apology—enlarging and embellishing it? Have you
ever found yourself trying to do something extra
for him or her? Yes. We all have. Why? Because we
find it so hard to transfer the basis of our confidence from ourselves to another person. That involves risk.

We find it much easier to trust in ourselves as
good repenters than in another person as a good
forgiver. Trusting another person involves the sur-
render of initiative; it breaks the pattern of my own
autonomy and control of the situation. It involves a
leap from safe ground to something unknown—the
other person's love and integrity. My own repentance, especially if it is accompanied by a kingsize
Coke as a peace offering, has much more substance
to me than her slender, "Forget it!" Those two
brief words of hers, furthermore, do not necessarily soothe my feelings; whereas a good, long, im-

possible-to-be-turned-down explanation and apology on my part will probably do a great deal for them.

Faith is not natural to us. We are not born with it, nor does it gracefully appear when we reach the age of accountability. Faith in the biblical sense of the term involves giving up our self-sufficiency and surrendering the satisfaction of feeling in control of the situation. This, above all else, is what we find hard to do.

Fight the Right Battle
The problem of unbelief affects guidance. God wants you and me to act moment by moment on the assumption that he is the Guide of our lives. Yet many Christians are distraught over finding the will of God, anxious about whether they have got it or not, calling up their friends to ask them for help, putting more and more slugs, as it were, into the vending machine and probably shaking and banging their fists at it in the meantime.

It is perfectly laudable to want to do the will of God—in fact, nothing is more important than doing the will of God—but the will of God is first and foremost to believe. It is tragic to waste our energies fighting a battle over guidance when we should be fighting a battle over faith. God has promised to be our Guide, so the thing for us to do is to step out on the assumption that we are being guided all the time, and that if ever we start veering off the track we shall hear that gentle voice in our ears saying, "This is the way; walk in it."

God has said he is the Forgiver; he has said he is the Guide, the Giver of love, the Convicter of sin, the One who holds and never loses the initiative, the Resurrection and the Life. He is the wonderful Counselor, the mighty God, the everlasting Father, the Prince of Peace, the One on whose shoulders is the government. Faith is acting in the light of who we know God to be, and then doing it at every point or moment in life. How wonderful then it is when we live this way habitually; when we come to the place where we regularly say "thank you" to God instead of "please." When we no longer try to persuade a "reluctant" God to dole out another helping of guidance or dispense another dose of patience in response to our eloquent or desperate pleas, then we have begun to see him as the One who guides us without pleading, the One who *is* patience and love and wisdom and strength, the One who has already done the work of atonement and redemption, the One whose kingdom *has* come.

Believing I Am Who I Am
The same Scriptures that tell me who God is tell me who I am, and if I am going to believe what they say about him, I have got to believe what they say about me. And what the Bible says about me is that I am not what I was. It says that something radical happened to me when I was born again. "If any one is in Christ, he is a new creation; the old has passed away, behold, the new has come" (2 Cor. 5:17). "I have been crucified with Christ; it is no longer I who live, but Christ who lives in me" (Gal. 2:20).

If we have been born again, we have been born of God's Spirit; we have been infused with his very life; we have been made partners of the divine nature; we are God's heirs, God's offspring. It is now our nature to want to do what God wants us to do. This was brought home to me once by a friend who said, "When I'm tempted, I stop to remember that a Christian can do whatever he wants to do."

I replied, "Now wait a minute. I thought that's just what a Christian couldn't do."

And then he said to me, "Do you *want* to be unloving? Do you *want* to be selfish? Do you *want* to be impure?"

Immediately I knew that what he had said was true. I did not want to be selfish; in fact, it was the last thing I wanted to be.

In John 15:4, Jesus said, "Abide in me" or "Remain in me." He was talking in the context of his being the vine and our being the branches. He was simply saying, "You are already joined to me; stay there. Be who you already are."

For part of one summer I worked on the maintenance crew at the Stony Brook School. One day a new employee came to work, a carpenter. I noticed immediately that he was behaving with unusual courtesy and respect, and my first reaction was that he was doing it to make a good impression so that he could be sure to keep his job. But the second and third day his behavior was the same, and I began to suspect that it wasn't just an act, and that maybe he was a Christian. So it proved to be.

True Christian behavior is not a means to an end. It is the expression of reality—of who we really are and of who God is. Too many Christians go around saying (to themselves, if not to others): "I'm hopeless." "I can't do it." "I'll never change." What are we actually communicating when we say those things? We are telling God that he is a liar. He has said that we are united to Christ, that Christ lives in us. And that is the Truth. What God has said about you and me is true, not what we may feel first thing in the morning.

Somebody once asked a wise and mature Christian woman how she was doing, and she said, "I'm better than I feel." Living the Christian life is living on the basis of who God is and who he has said you and I are in him.

So let me ask you, "What is your most besetting sin?"

Loving Father: Free to Do Wrong 2

The sonnet "Batter My Heart" was written in the early seventeenth century by John Donne. He started life as a courtier and young gallant, took part in a swashbuckling expedition to capture Spanish treasure in the port of Cadiz in 1596, ran off with the Lord Keeper's daughter—the Lord Keeper was in charge of all the Queen's money—and finally ended up as Dean of St. Paul's Cathedral and one of the most popular preachers of his day.

The sonnet begins with the cry "Batter my heart, three-personed God," and ends with these lines:

I am betrothed unto your enemy:
Divorce me, untie, or break that knot again,
Take me to you, imprison me, for I,

Except you enthrall me, never shall be free,
Nor ever chaste, except you ravish me.

The sentiments are stirring, and they find an echo
in almost all of us. We long for God to *do* something, even if it shakes us up. But God will never do
that. John Donne is asking God to do something
that God is just not going to do. God is not going to
batter our hearts; he is just not going to enthrall us,
imprison us or ravish us. As C. S. Lewis once said:
"God cannot ravish; he can only woo."

We find evidence of this in Scripture. The Incarnation teaches us this. The state of the world when
Christ was born seemed to demand an impressive
show of force on God's part. Things were in a sorry
mess, and the messengers God sent had repeatedly
been scorned or at best given only a polite hearing.
The state of affairs was such that God would surely
recommend shutting the world down for a couple of
centuries or putting an end to things with an atomic
explosion over Jerusalem. But that is not what God
did. Instead, he came to the world in weakness. He
allowed himself to be squeezed out of the inn by
more important guests and to be born in a dirty sta-
ble. He allowed himself to be dependent on a human being to wash him, feed him and clothe him.
He allowed himself to live and to die misunder-
stood, abused and unrecognized. Far from overwhelming the world, he seemed to be over-
whelmed by it. Violence and the battering of
human hearts had no place in his program. From
Madison Avenue's point of view, he was a total
failure.

Of course, God had done cataclysmic things on

occasion. He brought a flood on the earth. He called down fire and brimstone on Sodom and Gomorrah. He brought down plagues on Egypt. And we are led to believe that he will do more things like that as the end of the age approaches. But his greatest act of all to date was one of kindness and love.

No Lightning Bolts from God

God is secure in his control of each situation. He operates out of strength, not weakness. God does not have to panic and do something violent to get attention or give himself a sense of respect. God is strong enough to be able to appear weak.

Many of us, however, feel the way John Donne did. We want God to do something spectacular. We want God to batter our hearts to free us from our failures and jolt us out of our complacency. We want something violent to happen to ease us out of our dilemmas, and—let's admit it—to prove us right in the eyes of non-Christians. There are times when we get quite exasperated with God because he doesn't send down a blitzkrieg on all the rebellious and arrogant people around us who are flouting his standards. I get the impression that many non-Christians feel essentially the same way. "As soon as you hit me over the head, God, I'll start thinking about Christianity." "As soon as you prove yourself to me by some miraculous act, I'll believe. But it is your move, God." We all want the thrill of divine coup d'état. We want some spectacular action from God.

The reason God does not batter and enthrall and ravish and imprison us is *not* because he is satisfied

with us or with the status quo. It is not because he is
not interested in ousting the Enemy from our lives
or making us perfect. He is intensely interested in
that. The Scriptures could not be more explicit than
they are about God's ultimate purpose, which is to
have Jesus Christ at the center of everything; and
he is certainly not at the center of everything now.
But God is interested in the *way* this happens; he is
interested in the means as well as the end.

The means which God chooses hold incalculable
risks, as did the Incarnation. But God doesn't panic
the way we would.

God's way to change the world is what the Bible
calls the way of faith. One of these days God is
going to shake the heavens and the earth, as Isaiah
tells us. A day is coming when at the name of Jesus
every knee shall bow and every tongue confess that
Jesus Christ is Lord. But in the meantime, God is
saying to you and me: Will you voluntarily open
yourself up to me? Will you trust me? Will you decide on your own volition to operate your life on
the basis of my revelation of who I am and what I
have done?

In the previous chapter we defined faith: faith is
acting on the assumption that God is as good as his
Word. God is saying: I want to see if you will take
me at my Word.

Instead of overwhelming us with force, he wants
to win us with love.

Freedom to Choose

In the story of the prodigal son (Lk. 15:11-32), we
find a father who gave his sons *freedom to choose*.
When the younger son came and asked for his share

of the property, the father, apparently without hesitation, gave it to him. He would have gotten it in any case at his father's death, because under Jewish law a father was not free to leave his property to anyone he wanted; he was obliged to leave it to his sons. And it was by no means unusual for a father to distribute the estate before he died if he wished to retire from the actual management of affairs. But that is not what happened here. The son is calling for it himself before it is due. He is calling for his portion so he can collect the cash and get out from under his father's jurisdiction. And the father, we are told, *let him do it*. He gave the boy the property.

This is the way God is. God gives us freedom to make choices. He gives us freedom to choose even when he knows that what we are choosing is not the best and may even be the worst.

Now this doesn't mean, as some people might suggest, that God is permissive, that he doesn't have high standards, or that he doesn't care whether we do right or wrong. Far from it. God certainly does have standards—standards so high and holy, in fact, that they can only be kept by voluntary action. If a person were forced to keep them against his will, he would not in fact be keeping them at all, because they involve motives as well as outward actions. So the father allowed the son to go off, just as God allows us. If we choose to run away from him and indulge ourselves, he will let us. For us to stay against our will would never satisfy him.

The son squandered his inheritance and soon fell on bad times. There was a famine, and food was scarce, and the son sank to eating the food he was to feed to the swine. Finally, we're told the son "came to himself." That is an interesting phrase. It suggests that we are not really ourselves when we are estranged from God. You and I were made to be dependent on God, as our bodies were made to be dependent on food. Just as there is nothing weak and abnormal about eating food—in fact, it's distinctly abnormal not to—so there is nothing weak or abnormal about depending on God. In fact, only in this way will we really be ourselves and be complete people.

We are told that when the son came to himself and started home, his father saw him when he was still "at a distance"—the King James Version says "a great way off." Isn't that tremendous? The father was not just reluctantly taking in this wastrel son of his rather than turning him away. He was straining his eyes to see him! He was eagerly watching for him.

There is a marvelous hymn that says:

> *I sought the Lord, and afterward I knew*
> *He moved my soul to seek Him, seeking me; . . .*
>
> *I find, I walk, I love; but oh! the whole*
> *Of love is but my answer, Lord to Thee!*
> *For Thou wert long beforehand with my soul;*
> *Always Thou lovedst me.*

The father was "long beforehand" with the prodigal son. He was watching for him. When he saw him, he forgot all protocol and all the demands of dignity and propriety. The father *ran* to meet him.

The father didn't wait for his son's formal words of confession. He didn't wait till the son had cleaned himself up, even though he'd been wallowing in pigsties. The father embraced him and kissed him. When the son started his prepared speech, the father interrupted him and hollered to the servants: "Bring quickly the best robe, and put it on him; and put a ring on his hand, and shoes on his feet; and bring the fatted calf and kill it, and let us eat and make merry" (vv. 22-23).

Jesus is saying by this parable, "This is the way God is." When God sees us take that first willing step toward him, he doesn't wait for formal confessions or great penitential speeches. Even though we are still in our sins, wallowing in the mess we have made of our lives, he embraces us and takes us in. Someone has suggested that the robe in this story stands for honor (God clothes us with honor); the ring stands for authority (he gives us his name); the shoes stand for his according us sonship as opposed to servanthood. No making us second-rate members of his family because of the mess we have made of things. He takes us in as sons and daughters.

A God Who Pursues
What do we learn about the father's love from the way he related to his other son? Both sons were really lost: the first one in a foreign country, the second one behind a barricade of self-righteousness. Let me suggest that we are all either one or the other. The father does not take sides. He is just as concerned about the one son as about the other. Again he breaks protocol.

Think about the situation. The father has put on a feast to celebrate the younger son's return—his re-

birth. It has been the father's decision to celebrate.
It was done at his command and initiative. Then
here comes the older son. He has a jaundiced attitude even before he gets into the house. When he
first hears the sound of music and dancing, instead
of saying, "Hey, this sounds great; let's get in
there," he is immediately suspicious. He sends for
servants to find out what the story is. And then
when he hears the news he is angry, self-pitying
and resentful. He indulges in all sorts of surmises
that have no substance in truth at all. He disowns
his brother and then insults his father by calling him
"this son of yours."

I think that if I had been the father, I would have
let that older son stew in self-pity and miss the
party. I would not have demeaned myself by pleading for his approval of my decision. But the father
in this story is not like that. He went straight out
and begged the boy to come in. What incredible
love! *This,* says Jesus, is the way God is!

God's love is love that gives us freedom to
choose. It's love that strains to see the most distant
signs of our returning to him when we've wandered
away. It's love that never stands on ceremony, but
forgives fully and freely. It's love that embraces us
as we are in the midst of our foulness and filthiness.
It's love that gives us status with him, that makes us
part of his family, recipients of his Spirit. It's love
that breaks through the barriers of our self-righteousness and says to us in the midst of our pride:
"All that is mine is yours."

Do you believe that? At the moment of your
foulness, a foulness of sensual indulgence of phari-
saic arrogance, are you ready to be clothed with his

righteousness? When you hate yourself, are you willing to let him embrace you with his love?

Indwelling Spirit: Finding the Real You 3

W hat is hypocrisy? It is pretending to be other than you are. In Colossians 3 Paul gives us God's answer on living the Christian life, and it can be summed up in two statements: Don't be a hypocrite; be what you are.

We usually think of hypocrisy in terms of a person's pretending to be *better* than he or she is. But that is not the only kind of hypocrisy. The person who pretends to be *worse* than he or she is is just as much a hypocrite as the person who pretends to be better. The person who says he is dumb or ugly when he is not, is just as much a hypocrite as the person who exaggerates accomplishments. Likewise, the Christian who doesn't act like one is as much a hypocrite as the non-Christian who acts piously. Hypocrisy is pretending to be someone other than you are. To put it in more philosophical terms, hypocrisy is a lack of correspondence between appearance and reality in our lives.

In order to be who you are, you must first know who you are, and the problem with many of us is that we don't. We don't know the truth about ourselves. Here Paul's words are relevant. In Colossians 2, he said we (Paul is speaking to Christians here, of course) have died with Christ (v. 20). In chapter 3, he says that we have been raised with Christ (v. 1). That is who we are. We are people resurrected in Jesus. Paul says that this dying and rising again is an action completed in the past: we have died, and we have been raised again. That is a historical and spiritual reality. And we must live on the basis of that truth, not on the basis of any fantasies we may have.

We need to beware of living in fantasies, because fantasies are not real. I'm sure that we are all out of touch with reality to a certain extent, for who would claim to be totally sane? Only a madman, I think. But the closer to reality we are, the better. I knew of a husband and wife who had lived together for sixty or more years. When the man died, the woman was so used to having him around that she could not grasp the fact that he was gone. She would talk out loud to him as though he were still there; she would set a place for him at the table as she had for sixty years. Those of us who knew her would have rejoiced at any indication of her adjusting to reality, even though it would have brought her grief. If she had stopped talking out loud to him, we would have been glad, because we would have felt that she was finally beginning to face up to the facts.

One of the interesting things was that the way for her to find out about reality was not for her to consult her own feelings or look inside herself. Only someone else could tell her what was real.

Discovering the Truth about Yourself

Anyone who has had anything to do with ships and the sea knows that the only way to be sure whether or not you are making headway is to have some external mark by which to judge your position, whether it be a landmark or a star. If you simply look inside the boat, you cannot estimate your progress or position. If you simply look at the water around you, you cannot estimate your progress, either. You may be going with the tide, in which case you may seem hardly to be moving at all when in fact you are going fast. Or you may be going against the tide, in which case, though you appear to be moving fast through the water, you may be making little headway at all.

Several summers ago, I took my family to a place called Freedomland—a small, East-Coast version of Disneyland. I couldn't recommend the place, but there was one thing there that really fascinated me. It was a building called Casa Loca, meaning literally, "mad house." It consisted of a number of rooms all built at odd angles to the ground. Whole rooms were tilted. As a result, there were tables that looked level but which were so tilted that a book put down on them would slide off. In some rooms, there were lamps hanging from the ceiling. These obeyed the laws of gravity and hung straight down, while the whole room was tilted. So the lamps appeared to be *disobeying* the laws of gravity by hanging at a thirty-degree angle. Even water flowed "uphill."

The key to this deceptive environment was that the house had no windows. We couldn't see outside.

In order to safeguard ourselves from deception, we have to have an "outside," an objective point of reference. You and I are not going to find out what the reality concerning our new life in Christ is by grubbing around inside and analyzing our feelings. We will only find out by having God in his divine objectivity tell us. An interesting thing is that when we listen to him, we'll find something inside of us assenting to the fact that it is true. This is the mysterious and wonderful witness of the Spirit.

In Touch with Yourself

In chapter one I mentioned my friend who said that when he was tempted to do something wrong, he would ask himself, "Do I really *want* to be unloving? Do I really *want* to be selfish? Do I really *want* to be impure?" The answer always was, "I don't. In fact, that's the last thing I want to be. I never hate myself as much as when I'm being selfish or arrogant or impure, or whatever."

That is the witness of the Spirit to the truth that we have been crucified with Christ, and it is no longer we who live, but Christ who lives in us. Living the Christian life means living in accord with who God is and who he has said we are. We have seen that he has said he is the loving Father; now we see that we are in him, joined to him "one spirit." It's no longer we who live but Christ who lives in us.

Now this does not mean that our old life has no effect on us. It obviously does. The elderly woman who refused to admit the loss of her husband was still affected by him long after he died. In fact, her life was almost totally governed by him.

That is what Paul is dealing with in Colossians 2 and 3. Our present life should not, and need not, be governed by our old selves. Paul says, "Put to death therefore what is earthly in you." Start living in accordance with reality. He says that things like sexual immorality, impurity, passion, evil desires and greed (that strong desire within us that subordinates all other things) are part of the old you and me, not the new. That old self has been crucified with Christ; we do not have to live in accordance with it. In fact, it's pathetic when we do because we are living out of touch with reality. The old is an illusion, not a reality—though we seldom recognize our illusions as illusory.

Paul says, "Rid yourselves of all such things as these: anger, rage, malice, slander, and filthy language. . . . Do not lie to each other, since you have taken off your old self with its practices and have put on the new self" (Col. 3:8-10 NIV).

Note the logic Paul uses here. He does not say, "Do not lie to one another because it leads to trouble and breaks relationships, and because we cannot live as a community if we are not open with one another." All these things are true, but he uses a far more compelling and profound logic. He says, "Do not lie to one another because that is not the real you. You would be a hypocrite if you were to lie.

You would be a hypocrite if you were to use abusive language. You would be a hypocrite if you were to engage in dirty talk."

This passage is calling for a totally new way of life—not because we have looked around at all the life-styles and selected this one, like choosing a suit off a store rack, but because this is *us*. Only it is not us, but Christ. We are now part of him. We have been united to Christ, made one in spirit. What Paul is saying is that there is a spiritual reality that already constitutes a compelling reason for us to act in accordance with it, to act congruously. When God's grace and our faith first met, a new being came into existence. A new self was born from that sacred intercourse, and it is now a primary reality in God's eyes. Granted, this self has not yet been fully realized in the fabric of our daily living, but its very existence constitutes a compelling reason for behaving in a certain way.

This spiritual reality is ultimate—it is more real than what appears—and the more real must logically and sensibly take precedence over the less real. You and I *have been* united to Jesus Christ. We have been crucified with him, and it is no longer we who live but Christ who lives in us. This is the greatest reality in the universe as far as we are concerned, and its very existence constrains us to behave in a certain way. Among other things, it constrains us not to lie, because Jesus Christ does not lie. And we have been joined to him.

My new identity calls me to be pure, compassionate, kind, humble, gentle, patient, forgiving, truthful and loving. To be anything else would be hypocritical.

We have another example of this same principle in 1 Corinthians 1:10-13, where Paul commands the church to be united. The reason for this command is that Jesus is not divided, and we are part of him. The ultimate reality is that I have been joined to you in one body—whether you like it or not—by virtue of the fact that we have both been born again and so joined to Christ. This puts us under the logical compulsion to be united in our daily lives.

The New Testament does not simply instruct us not to tell lies, not to indulge in sexual immorality and not to give in to evil desires, greed and slander because we ought not to; it does not simply tell us to be united because we ought to be. It gives us the logical reason of an appeal to congruity—to make what *appears* conform to what *is*.

This means that God will never countenance cultural or economic divisions between Christians. If we make such distinctions we are hypocrites; we are out of touch with reality. If I am a Christian, I am united to Christ and so is every other born-again Christian; black, white, rich, poor, educated or illiterate. God has made us one in the most dynamic way that ever could be imagined, by putting us to death and raising us together in Christ. Truth calls us to live in union with our brothers and sisters, and Christ enables us to do this because he is our life.

Keeping Priorities Straight
In Colossians 2-3, Paul points out that the life-style that was chosen for us when we were united to Christ is not a matter of wearing particular clothes, or having our hair a particular length, or going to

bed early, or staying up late, or being placid and
quiet instead of vivacious and noisy. These things
are peripheral and secondary. Life in Christ has to
do with compassion, kindness, humility, gentleness
and patience; with bearing with one another and
forgiving one another. This life is concerned with
love, which is like an outer garment that holds the
other characteristics in place. I wish that when we
talk about life-style, we could think about these
matters of heart rather than about superficial values
and attitudes.

You may be asking: Why does Paul need to tell
us to put these things on if we already have them in
Christ? Why does he tell us to put to death whatever belongs to our earthly nature if it's already
dead? The answer is what I suggested at the beginning: that we do not always act according to who
we are. We forget. And furthermore, most of us are
so subject to peer pressure that we act like chame-
leons: we change color according to our environment. The sad fact is that we listen to all the lies
being spoken around us, and we believe many of
them. These lies say that it's courageous to retaliate; that it's weak to turn the other cheek; that it's
stupid not to lie to get out of a jam; that it's foolish
to let others walk all over you; that it's fun to be a
smart aleck; and that it's only right to save your
own skin.

Because we so often forget who we are, and because we are so subject to peer pressure, Paul has
to remind us to *be what we are*. Thus he closes this
section of his letter by urging us to spend time with
one another. As we teach and counsel each other
wisely, and as we sing psalms and hymns together,

God's truth will be brought home to our hearts and minds again, and we will reaffirm who we are.

Don't be a hypocrite: be who you are! God has provided all you need for life and godliness; he has made you a participant in his divine Spirit. Act according to God's *fact*. Take him at his Word. That is faith.

Lord:
Living in Touch
with the Truth

4

I think we have all at some time or another had the uncomfortable experience of discovering that certain assumptions we had been living under were not valid. It can be very disconcerting to find that something we thought was true was not.

I visited the Middle East once, and one of the places I went to was Istanbul. I arrived after dark and took a taxi into the city. Now one of the assumptions I had always lived under is that when you see a red traffic light, you stop. But not so in Istanbul. Red light or green, my taxi driver went straight through every intersection. Maybe he slowed down a fraction, especially if there was a particularly large Mercedes truck coming from one side or the other. But stop he did not. This was a little disconcerting. It upset one of my basic assumptions, as well as my nervous system.

Another basic assumption of mine was that the female sex was more or less equal to the male—worthy of the same respect and the same privileges. But in Saudi Arabia I found how wrong I was. Women there wear veils when they go out in public; they walk a few feet behind their husbands; and they're not allowed to drive cars. (What I can't understand is why the accident rate in Riyadh is so high.) When Queen Elizabeth visited there a few years ago, she was made an *honorary man*, so she could appear in public with the king. But I found it all disconcerting; these assumptions I had taken for granted were not regarded as true in the Middle East.

In these cases it didn't make much difference, because in Istanbul in spite of going through red lights my taxi driver got me to the hotel safely; and my wife wasn't with me in Saudi Arabia.

But there is one basic assumption that does matter, and it affects all of us whether we live in Istanbul, Saudi Arabia, Kenya, China or Peru. This is a basic assumption that is universally true because God has declared it to be so; and it has enormous consequences for us in this life and in the life to come. Whether or not you find in disconcerting will depend on whether you have recognized it before or not. In chapters three and four we looked at how we must live our lives congruently with the knowledge that God is our loving Father and Indwelling Spirit. Here we will look at life lived in accord with the truth that Jesus Christ is Lord.

Lord of All

In Philippians 2:9-13, we read:

> *God has highly exalted him and bestowed on him the name which is above every name, that at the name of Jesus every knee should bow, in heaven and on earth and under the earth, and every tongue confess that Jesus Christ is Lord, to the glory of God the Father.*
>
> *Therefore, my beloved, as you have always obeyed, so now, not only as in my presence but much more in my absence, work out your own salvation with fear and trembling; for God is at work in you, both to will and work for his good pleasure.*

Note that the text does not say that Jesus *should* be or *ought* to be Lord, but that he already is. There is nothing conditional about this. Sometimes in churches we hear people talking about "making Jesus Christ Lord." That kind of talk can be misleading. Jesus is not up for election, as though we could cast our vote, as it were, and put him over the top! He is not running for Lord, nor is this world a democracy, ruled by popular vote.

Jesus Christ *is* Lord. It has already been decided. God the Father, the Creator, the Beginning and the End has made Jesus Christ Lord, and that means that his lordship is an underlying assumption that all creation at some point is going to have to reckon with. The wonderful thing is that we can come to terms with it now, and so begin even in this life to live in touch with the truth.

What does it mean that Jesus is Lord? It means that he is the One who has the last word. It means that he is the One who has the right and the authority to be the determiner of right and wrong. It means that he is the One who should rule our choices. It means that he is the One to whom we should be servants, and he is the One who has the right to determine the circumstances of our lives.

It is not just an accident that you were born into your particular family; that you have the particular body you have; that you live next door to the particular neighbors you do; that you are in the particular situation at work that you are in; that you have the particular roommate you do. God has made us the way we are and placed us where we are. Most of us have things about ourselves that we don't like— probably for good reasons. But if Jesus Christ is Lord, then we need to start doing what he has told us to do, which is to "give thanks in all circumstances; for this is the will of God in Christ Jesus for you" (1 Thess. 5:18). This is not to say that God is the immediate cause of tragedy in our lives, but that through his lordship we can have victory over all our circumstances. A long time ago I felt God's Spirit convicting me when I complained about things like being served food I disliked, and not being six inches taller than I am, and not being as good a tennis player as I'd like to be. Things like this Jesus decided, and he is Lord.

While we can't choose who our parents will be, nor what century we'll be born in, nor whether we'll be tall or short, nor whether we'll have cancer next year, on the really important issues (and I mean what I say), we are free to choose, and nothing can deprive us of that freedom. No person, no government, no system, no law can ever deprive you or me of the power to choose whether to love our neighbors or to hate them, whether to be selfish or unselfish, whether to tell a lie or to tell the truth, whether to be happy or miserable, whether to fight social ills or be complacent about them, whether to say something kind or cut somebody down, whether to retaliate or to turn the other cheek, whether to be cynical or constructive, jealous or generous. No person can ever deprive us of the right of choice in these things. Only God can and he never will. These are the things that really matter: love and hate, justice and injustice, pride and humility, selfishness and selflessness; not the outward things but the inward things; not the circumstances of life, but the kind of people we are *in* those circumstances.

People sometimes ask me whether I'm glad I decided to settle in this country after having been raised in England—whether I prefer life here or there. I never know what to say because it's such an irrelevant question: what matters is the quality of life, not the location. And the quality is determined mostly by you and me, and by the attitudes we choose to adopt. It is what goes on inside of us, the choices that we make, that determine what our relationships are like and whether life has satisfaction and meaning and significance for us. It is this power to choose that really makes us men and women. This is what makes us the highest of all God's creatures.

The fact that Jesus Christ is Lord means that he has the right to be the determiner of our choices, the One upon whose "Yes" or "No" we decide to act. Whoever or whatever determines my choice at any time is, ipso facto, LORD of my life at that moment. The question is: Am I going to live in touch with the truth or not, as though Jesus were Lord (which he is) or not?

A Bully in Every Crowd

Sometimes we let others govern our choices. How many times have you been caught in a traffic jam? Neither you nor anybody else has moved for five minutes, because there's nowhere to go. There are two things you can do: keep your impatience under control or give vent to it. Maybe you keep your temper under control, but Mr. Jones (and that's the right name for him) behind you starts blowing his useless horn. Then you start doing exactly the same thing. You didn't have to; you let another person determine your behavior, and at that moment he was the lord of your life.

Take another example. You're standing in a circle, and someone starts boasting about what she's done or bought or said or seen, and everyone else starts following suit, trying to outdo the previous speaker. Deep in your heart you despise this. You can't love this miserable, endlessly unsatisfying game of one-upmanship. You know it's as empty as the moon, but you do it, probably embellishing your own story along the way. Why? Because you let yourself be ruled by what the others are doing. And at that moment they are lords over you.

But it's not just the things that everybody else is doing that we let rule us. It's often our fears: fears of being rejected, fears of being left out, fears of not pleasing other people, fears of being different. I still remember vividly an experience I had when I was in prep school in England. It was during World

War 2, and our food was rationed. Each of us had our own little jars of butter and sugar on the tables in the dining hall. The butter ration was about an eighth of a pound a week, and the sugar about half or three-quarters of a cup—for everything! The jars got filled up each Monday morning. One day there were a bunch of us at a table, and neither the teacher nor student-prefect in charge turned up. There we were, left to our own devices. Someone said, "Let's take some of their butter and sugar." Fearing ridicule for being such a prig, I took some of the prefect's sugar. I let fear rule me, and at that moment it became my lord.

Now God redeemed that situation, because he loves to redeem. He impregnated my conscience with his will and wisdom, and I heard a small, insistent voice repeating, "Confess to Michael" (the student-prefect), "Confess to Michael." For a while I tried to silence the voice because the task seemed horrendous. I was a sophomore, and known to be a Christian, and I was going to have to go to a senior and tell him that I had stolen some of his sugar and ask him to forgive me. It wouldn't have been right to try to make a joke of it. Nor would it have been right to think that because I'd only taken a little it really didn't matter. All I could hear inside was, "Confess to Michael." Finally I did; I let Jesus rule me instead of fear.

Thomas Merton wrote in *The Seven-Story Mountain*, "There is only one happiness; to please Him. Only one sorrow, to be displeasing to Him and to refuse Him something, to turn away from Him even in the slightest thing, even in thought, in a half-willed movement of appetite." The moment I walked through the door of doing what God wanted me to do, of acknowledging Jesus as Lord, I was immediately enclosed in the four walls of a new and glorious kind of freedom, the freedom that floods the soul when it worships God and him alone.

Some of us are ruled not by others or the fear they create but by our own guilt. We have sinned, and because we are not each moment believing God for his forgiveness, we are still carrying around feelings of guilt. Those feelings of guilt time and again raise their ugly heads, and we let them determine a decision. You remember what David did when he had committed adultery with Bathsheba. Instead of confessing his guilt and asking forgiveness, he let guilt rule him. He tried first to manipulate and then to get rid of the one whose presence made him feel guilty and whose absence, he thought, would free him. Have you ever let your guilty feelings drive you into lying and deceit?

There are a thousand things within and without us that we let rule us: our good looks (or, as we think, our bad looks); our passions and appetites (have you ever been ruled by a cookie or a dish of ice cream?); our love of things, of cars, clothes, stereos, record albums.

None of these things is wrong in itself. The only question is whether they rule us, whether at any moment of any day a decision we make is determined by them rather than by what we know God wants us to do. Have you ever let shame of Christ and of confessing him publicly rule your heart? Have you bowed down to the god of fear and shame? There is a hymn that speaks of this:

*Jesus, and shall it ever be, a mortal man
    ashamed of Thee?*
*Ashamed of Thee whom angels praise, Whose
    glories shine through endless days?*
*Ashamed of Jesus! Just as soon let midnight be
    ashamed of noon;*
*'Tis midnight with my soul till He, Bright morn-
    ing star, bid darkness flee.*
*Ashamed of Jesus! That dear friend on whom my
    hopes of heaven depend!*
*No; when I blush be this my shame, That I no
    more revere His name.*

To Serve Is to Be Free

Have you agreed with God about whom you will
serve? Most of us end up serving ourselves most of
the time. We hear talk suggesting that we should
free ourselves from responsibilities so that we can
"find ourselves." We hear that we must look out for
number one. But life will never work properly so
long as we are serving ourselves. The happiest people I know—in fact, the only happy people I
know—are people who have lost themselves in the
service of others. We were made by God to have a
vocation; that is, a "calling," and that calling, if we
get it from God instead of from the world, will always be a calling to serve others. Do not listen to
what the world tells you about what to do with your
life, because what the world tells you will be
wrapped up with moneymaking and indulgence.
Listen to what God wants you to do.

Agree with Jesus about your circumstances,
your choices, and life will begin to make sense.
You will be operating on the basis of a truly valid

assumption, namely, that Jesus Christ is Lord. And this, in fact, is walking by faith because it is acting on the assumption that God is as good as his Word.

"God has made him both Lord and Christ, this Jesus whom you crucified" (Acts 2:36).

Initiator/Completer: 5
Whose Move Is It?

Some of you—the initiated ones, the happy few—are familiar enough with Winnie-the-Pooh to recall something that Eeyore once said to him: "They're funny things, Accidents. You never have them till you're having them."

I would like to suggest that what A.A. Milne's melancholy philosopher said about accidents is also true—strangely enough—about our vital experiences with God: we don't have them until we are having them. Nobody can lay out a series of drills which, if conscientiously followed now, will guarantee communion with God sometime in the future.

You see, God happens to us; not the other way around.

"Don't Stupid Yourself"

When she was small, our daughter had a habit
(which we teased her about) of turning passive
verbs into active ones. (I am not sure whether she
was aware of the grammatical function that she was
performing, but that is beside the point.) Instead of
talking about "being made nervous," she would
talk about "nervousing" herself. Once when her
mother was about to try on a wig, she said,
"Mother, don't stupid yourself."

But we cannot change the voice of the verb as far
as God is concerned. That is what Moses tried to do
in Exodus 3 and 4. God appeared to him in the
burning bush and told Moses that he was God's
chosen instrument to lead the Israelites out of slav-
ery in Egypt. When Moses replied by making excuses, he was thinking that he held the initiative. So
not only did he nervous himself, but he stupided
himself also.

In reality the action was altogether God's, not
Moses'. God had started it, and God would finish
it. This was clear enough to Moses at the very beginning, but he quickly lost sight of it. It was obviously God who called to him out of the burning
bush. There could be no question about that. Moses
was on a perfectly routine shepherding maneuver,
and I am sure that no one was more surprised than
he when God's call came. But almost immediately—because he was human—he forgot the truth
about God, and he thought that everything from
then on depended on him. He forgot that it is in the
nature of God not only to initiate but also to sustain
and to follow through on what he starts. He forgot
that it was not Moses who was going to lead the

children of Israel out of Egypt with the help of God, but God who was going to lead them out by the hand of Moses. That's why he got flustered and worried. That's why you and I get flustered and worried too.

In previous chapters we have looked at God as Lover, Indweller and Lord. Now we will see him as Initiator and Completer. Because Moses had forgotten that God is the great Initiator and Completer, he started asking questions and making excuses.

Moses' first objection was, "Who am I? Why was I chosen? What makes me fit for the job?" He was worried about failure, though he obviously had some of the qualifications needed. He had the right background: he had been raised in Pharaoh's court; he had the right social credentials. But he had made a mess of his relationships and had ended up running away from the situation.

What was God's answer to him? "I will be with you" (Exodus 3:12). That was what mattered. At this point it was largely irrelevant even that Moses could be forgiven and cleansed from the past—wonderful as that was. What mattered was who was in control. And God's reminder to Moses was, "I am." "I, whose glory shines here in the burning bush; I, who am as unimpaired by the passing of time as this bush is by the burning of the fire; I, who am as independent of sustenance or fuel as that steadily burning fire. This is my business. Certainly, I will be with you."

Something of this kind, it seems to me, is what God wants to say to us today. Days break very differently upon us, but nothing can separate us from the love of God—the love of God as a happening;

not as a theory learned in the past but as a very present experience.

So Moses' first objection ("Who am I?") was not valid. God had promised to be with him and to be his life.

His second excuse was his inability to answer if he were asked the name of God: "If I come to the people of Israel and say to them, 'The God of your fathers has sent me to you,' and they ask me, 'What is his name?' what shall I say to them?" (Ex. 3:13). He was using his theological illiteracy as an excuse. But listen to God's answer: "I AM WHO I AM. . . . Say this to the people of Israel, 'I AM has sent me to you'" (3:14). No course in theology ever equipped anyone to give an answer like that. The answer lies not in the words but in the divine revelation in the midst of life's suffering that God *is* and is himself. If this is believed, it will deliver us.

Moses' third excuse to God was that the people would not believe him or listen to him. God graciously met this excuse by showing him miracles he could perform in Egypt. And the miracles contained great significance for Moses himself: a simple shepherd's crook rather than a monarch's golden scepter was what God was going to use to put the Egyptians to flight (Ex. 4:2-4). Then there was the matter of his hand being made leprous and then clean again (4:6-7). Surely this spoke of God's ability to meet Moses' consciousness of moral failure with forgiving grace. Third, in the water of the Nile becoming blood (4:9), there was for Moses a great reassurance of God's judgment on Egypt.

But the main point was not the lessons that these acts taught Moses, but the fact that they were miraculous: they were done by God, and they were to be performed again before the Egyptians.

Thus, adequacy is not a matter of training. You cannot practice God's miracles for him ahead of time so that they'll happen right when you need them. The lesson is that we are to thank God for, and to take courage from, the supernatural things he is doing in our lives *now*; and we are to count on his doing them again and again in the future in the presence of others. An unbelieving friend is going to be impressed most not by reports of what happened last week or last year to somebody else, but by the changes in your life and mine that he sees before his own eyes and that can be explained by nothing except God.

In his last excuse, Moses complained of his lack of eloquence: "I am slow of speech and of tongue," he said (4:10). God met him with a promise: "Who has made man's mouth? Who makes him dumb, or deaf, or seeing, or blind? Is it not I, the LORD? Now therefore go, and I will be with your mouth and teach you what you will speak" (4:11-12). Unfortunately, Moses didn't believe the promise, and God ended the conference by saying that he would send Aaron to do the talking. But it was also Aaron who later shaped the golden calf.

Living Tomorrow Today
What is God saying to us today? He is certainly not saying that it doesn't matter what you and I do. He is not saying that the development of habits of prayer and Bible study are not important. They obviously are. But I believe he is saying that we had

better recognize that, spiritually, today is tomorrow.

Years ago at an Inter-Varsity conference, I was struck by a speaker who came at us again and again with the thought, "As now—so then." "What makes you think," this man would say, "that you are going to be any different tomorrow from what you are today? Do you think that going across the ocean to a foreign mission field is going to make you any different from what you are here and now? If you are not a missionary here at home today, you are not going to be one on the mission field tomorrow."

The game has started. Play has already begun. Communion with God is now or never. It is only as we love him today that we will ever love him.

So Moses did not lead the children of Israel out of Egypt by his skill and God's help; God led them out of Egypt by the hand of Moses. But didn't Moses have things to do too? Was he just a passive tool?

"God helps those who help themselves." That's a common saying, and it is usually considered to be common sense. I think I like it, but it is one of those sayings about which I have a slightly uneasy feeling. It could so very easily carry with it the connotation that God is the big booster who comes to the rescue when our resources are not quite equal to the task, the extra horsepower that gives us the margin of safety, God underwriting our enterprises. And that is a blasphemous view of God. God does not tag along with us. God is the great Initiator. He is the beginning as well as the end, and he never lets the initiative out of his hands. He would not be God if he did. One of the great heresies the early church had to combat was that God had wound up the universe and then left it to go ticking along on its own. If the Bible from beginning to end says anything, it says that our God is the living God, alive and active today. To say that God helps those who help themselves is dangerously close, it seems to me, to saying that God is the pump that lifts the water once we have primed it and provided we keep moving the handle up and down.

But to reject the statement seems wrong too. Am I supposed to sit back and take it easy, relax and wait for the proverbial bolt from the blue? This doesn't sound like that great spiritual competitor Paul, fighting to win, running the race and finishing his course. Nor does it seem to fit the New Testament exhortations to "fight the good fight" and to "lay hold of life."

In the Driver's Seat?
This issue of "How much does God do and how much do I do?" is not an abstract one. It invades every area of our lives. Take evangelism, for example. Is the burden of responsibility for the evangelization of the world really on our shoulders? If so, shouldn't I as a Christian feel an urgent obligation to make an evangelistic occasion out of every encounter? Or should I wait for God to "lead" me to speak? If I do the former, how do I know that this isn't an effort of "the flesh" which the New Testament condemns? If I do the latter, how do I know that I am not just being lazy or just rationalizing myself out of a worthy but rather embarrassing responsibility? These are real questions for us.

Take the whole matter of prayer. Some of our
friends tell us that all that's needed to see more
people converted, the sick healed, and so on, is
more prayer. They quote the verse: "You do not
have, because you do not ask" (James 4:2). But
doesn't this sound alarmingly like our being in the
driver's seat? As though another human being's
eternal welfare rests on my time in prayer? Taken
seriously, this puts upon us an altogether too awe-
some responsibility. Furthermore, I believe that if
we followed this view to its logical conclusion, it
would turn prayer into the most unbearable drudgery. I cannot believe that the God of the Bible
would ever be the author of unbearable drudgery.

What is the solution to this problem? In Colossians 1:24-29, Paul is speaking of his evangelistic
activities, his preaching of the gospel. In verse 29,
he says, "For this I toil, striving with all the energy
which he mightily inspires within me." I believe
that here we have the resolution of the apparent
conflict that lies before us, and I believe it is a resolution that lies in the very nature of the gospel.

What is the nature of the gospel? The old covenant was lifeless. In response to their faith, God
placed upon his people the seal of ownership, and
he undertook to order and control their destiny. He
showed himself constantly solicitous of their welfare and concerned for their good. He imparted his
Spirit in special ways to special people like Moses,
the judges, and the prophets. But the children of
Israel as a whole were more like his possession than
they were his sons.

The new covenant is different. Paul in Colossians talks of the new covenant as "the mystery

hidden for ages and generations but now made manifest to his saints" (1:26). It is nothing less than "Christ in you, the hope of glory" (1:27). Christ, who is the manna of God, is no longer rationed out to us, but has come to live his very life within us. There is within us a well of water springing up into everlasting life. This is the gospel. Yet few of us who call ourselves Christians seem to recognize, let alone to enjoy, the truth of this.

This was the message that utterly captivated Paul, that so completely transformed Peter, and that made of a tiny handful of very ordinary folk the revolutionaries that turned the world of their day upside down. It was this message, that a totally new dimension of living had been opened up by God's initiative, that they proclaimed. God's life—life possessed within itself of creative love and healing, pulsating with the power of spiritual and moral renewal—is what the gospel is all about. It is not a new "help yourself" message.

We need no longer be slaves, confronted on the outside with the injunctions of our master; we can now be sons and daughters, imbued from within with the characteristic life of our Father. No wonder Paul could not wait to pass it on! The gospel does not offer people a new philosophy of life; it does not offer them a new party to join, a new theology to embrace, or a new set of works to perform. It offers them a totally new life to possess the innermost recesses of their being. Healing from within.

This is the nature of the gospel. Here we will find the resolution to the problem of our initiative and God's.

I believe that sometimes our emphasis on the holiness and otherness of God on the one hand, and on our own sinfulness on the other, has led us to an overly suspicious approach to our "natural" inclinations and enthusiasms. I do not believe that Paul thought of the injunctions of God as always coming to him from the outside, of the will of God as being imposed on him through an external obligation. No! His grasp of the gospel message was far too strong. He knew that Christ was his life, that it was no longer he who lived but Christ who lived in him. Unless this is true, all the New Testament's boastful talk of freedom is a mockery.

Freedom is doing whatever you want to do. And that is precisely what the Christian can do, because what he or she wants to do, really *wants* to do, is the will of God. Do you really want to be unloving? Do you really want to be spiteful? No. If we truly believe, we have a mighty inspiration within. "Whoever drinks of the water that I shall give him will never thirst; the water that I shall give him will become in him a spring of water welling up to eternal life" (John 4:14). "For this I toil, striving with all the energy that he mightily inspires within me" (Col. 1:29).

If we do not think we are experiencing the mighty inspiration within, it is because we are not believing.

Let us discover what it means to live knowing that God is the Initiator and Completer. Let us *expect* the constant welling up of his Spirit within us; his Spirit, which, by his grace, has become our spirit, doing his work in his way.

Dr. A. W. Tozer summarized the whole encounter between Moses and God by leaning over the pulpit saying, "And God finally said to Moses, 'Moses! It doesn't matter who you are. I AM!'" God wants us to reverse that deadly sequence that was started by the Fall when a man and woman grasped at the initiative for themselves and chose to lead instead of follow God. He wants us to see that there is no power vacuum that we have to fill. God wants us to believe that he is at work today, that he is the living God alive today, prompting, initiating, leading and acting. God wants us to know that he is light and life, truth and hope, love, joy, and judgment. Our part is simply to take him at his Word, rest in his initiative, and so become the most passive activists and the most active pacifists the world has ever seen.

The union of Christ and his church: it is a mystery, but it is a very real experience for you and me every hour that we believe him and let him live out his life in us.

Guide: Walking in His Will 6

F aith is acting on the basis of who God is. In previous chapters we've looked at God as Lover, Provider, Lord, Initiator and Completer. He is also our Guide. The word *guide* is used again and again in Scripture:

He will be our guide *for ever (Ps. 48:14).*

The meek he will guide *in judgment (Ps. 25:9).*

You guide *me with your counsel and afterward you will take me into glory (Ps. 73:24).*

The Lord will guide *you continually (Isaiah 58:11).*

When the Spirit of truth comes, he will guide *you into all truth (John 16:13).*

In addition, the concept of guidance is reiterated through Scripture in terms such as:

The Lord shall direct *your paths (Prov. 3:6).*
I will lead *the blind by ways they have not known
    (Isaiah 42:16).*
Counsel *and sound judgment are mine, says the
    Lord (Prov. 8:14).*

Furthermore, in scores of analogies, the Lord is described as: Counselor (Isaiah 9:6), Teacher (John 3:2), Light (Ps. 27:1), Captain (2 Chron. 13:12; Hebrews 2:10), Shepherd (Ps. 23; John 10), Father (Luke 11:2, Eph. 4:6), Husband (Hosea 2:7; Isaiah 54:5).

Finally, we are given example after example in Scripture of the Lord's guiding individuals. And down through the centuries Christian people have affirmed the fact that God has indeed been their Guide.

I think it is important to understand clearly what Scripture means here, so that we do not force *our* meaning into the Word of God. It is all too easy to do this because of cultural and language barriers, as well as our tendency to make things say what we want them to say.

In connection with guidance, we must be careful not to ask God to do something for us or be something to us that he has no intention of doing or being. God does not want a lot of little robots running around. In *The Screwtape Letters* by C. S. Lewis, the devil Wormwood deplores the (from his point of view) appalling truth that God "really *does* want to fill the universe with a lot of loathsome little replicas of Himself—creatures whose life, on its miniature scale, will be qualitatively like His own, not because He has absorbed them but because their wills freely conform to His. *We* want cattle who can finally become food; *He* wants servants who can finally become sons."

No Strings Attached
God has accorded us the dignity of choice. He wants people who will love him of their own free will. True love, of course, cannot exist except in the context of the possibility of hate. If I had no option but to love my coworker, Jim, there would be no virtue in my love. It would no longer be *love*. It is only because I could *hate* him that I can love him.

Similarly, if I have no option but to trust, if I am programmed to do it, there is no virtue in it; it is no longer trust. God will never demean us by taking away our free will.

God's purpose is to have a lot of lovers and trusters, and anything he does about guiding us will be in line with that purpose and subordinate to it. Thus a "blueprint" type of guidance will be the exception, not the rule. To be told, "Jim, you are to marry Nancy," will be very unusual. I won't say that it will never happen, but it is highly unlikely. Why? Because, compared with whether Jim trusts and loves God moment by moment and trusts and loves Nancy moment by moment, the choice of Nancy or someone else is virtually inconsequential. The will of God has primarily to do with who Jim is every second—what his thoughts, actions, attitudes and words are. And it may be that Jim can be all that God wants him to be whether he's married to Nancy or to someone else.

Too many people marry the person that they are convinced God wants them to marry and then turn around and respond to that person out of complete selfishness. No matter who your spouse is, if you are acting selfishly you are outside the will of God. God's will is plain in that situation.

For John Avery or Melissa Mellinger to be told in so many words to go to Tegucigalpa as a missionary with Latin America Mission would be abnormal. If that happened, he or she would be tempted to proceed in self-sufficiency. Compared with whether John and Melissa are acting moment by moment on the assumption that God is a loving Father, that he is the Indwelling Spirit who prompts holiness, that he is the great Initiator, the Lord and so on, it is virtually inconsequential whether John and Melissa are missionaries in Tegucigalpa or teachers in Louisville or doctors in Cleveland.

There *may* be occasions when having a clear blueprint will stimulate greater faith and love than not having one. In that case, God will give it; but that is not usually the case.

From God's point of view, his guidance of us is far more akin to the exercise of fatherly responsibility than it is to anything else. Good fathers give very few specific orders to their kids, especially older ones. Fathers lay down parameters and principles and hope their kids will act on their own within those guidelines and parameters. In fact, parents ought to get worried if their children are constantly coming and saying, "Is this okay?" "Do you think I should go out with Mark?" "Do you want me to wear this suit or that one?" Such dependence in an older child would be neurotic.

God has laid down his parameters. They are in Scripture. He has given us everything we need for the re-education of our minds and the adjustment of our values. He has provided clear principles to guide us in many areas, including:

-*what kinds of things we should think about*
-*what we should wear*
-*how we should spend our money*
-*what we should do about our sexual urges*
-*what our attitude should be toward marriage*
-*how we should relate to our bosses or teachers*
-*what our attitude should be toward the problem of a career*
-*how we should respond to fellow believers*
-*how we should treat our parents*
-*how we should treat the poor, widows and refugees*
-*what we should do about commitments we have made*
-*what we should do about injustices in society*

An Ongoing Concern

God has also undertaken to watch over us moment by moment and let us know clearly if, at any time, we start veering off to the right or left. Isaiah 30:21 says: "Whether you turn to the right or to the left, your ears will hear a voice behind you, saying, 'This is the way; walk in it'" (NIV). If God is straining his eyes for any sign that the wandering, disobedient prodigal son is turning around, how much more is he going to be watching us constantly?

A good friend of mine living in India had some decisions to make about his future. He was an obedient and trusting Christian, but, like the rest of us, went through periods of doubt. During one of these periods he went out for a walk and came upon an old, dilapidated church building which he decided to explore. As he crossed the threshold, something fell at his feet from the rafters. It was a dead bird. Immediately, God's truth sprang to his mind: "Are not two sparrows sold for a penny? And not one of them will fall to the ground without your Father's will. . . . Fear not, therefore; you are of more value than many sparrows" (Matthew 10:29, 31).

God is infinitely more concerned than you and I that we walk in his ways, fulfill his highest purposes for our lives and be of the greatest use in his kingdom. He is going to do everything he possibly can, short of coercing us, to see that we are everything he wants us to be. Some of us are still thinking of him as an ogre, hiding around the corner, waiting for us to transgress his will so that he can pounce on us and clap us into jail. Nothing could be further from the truth.

A father with even the meagerest kind of love for his children will say, "Watch out, Billie, that's hot." If a human father can show that kind of love, how much more will the Lord let us know if we are approaching danger or straying from the path. He is not going to give us the warning in veiled, enigmatic, cryptic, equivocal terms, but clearly, simply, in a way we can understand and follow.

The voice of God will always come clearly, definitely, insistently, and quietly. God is not going to tantalize us by speaking in riddles. If he has a point to make, he will make it in a clear-cut way and he will go on making it until we comprehend (though comprehending, we may choose to disobey). When God had a message for the people of Israel, did he mince words? No. The prophets spoke without hesitation or equivocation. But the people chose not to listen.

I believe that this is what God means when he says that he will guide us continually, that he will lead us to the truth, that he will be our Shepherd. A shepherd does not gather the sheep around him in the morning and say, "Take the first gate on the right and turn left. After half a mile, take the left fork to the second rock." God says, "Follow your noses. Do what comes naturally to you [and we know what *naturally* means for the Christian]. If you start veering off to one side or the other, I'll come after you."

Romans 8:14 says, "For all who are led by the Spirit of God are sons of God." You cannot separate being "led by the Spirit of God" from a walk in faith. Paul equates these two things in Galatians 3. To be led by the Spirit is to walk in faith, and to walk in faith is to be led by the Spirit.

One Ear to the Ground
Being led by faith does, however, involve listening and sensitivity—listening to the positive and negative things God may be saying. If you feel led by faith (by the Spirit) to take some action or other, how can you be sure that this guidance is from God? How can you sure you are not simply rationalizing your own selfish desires?

First, God's guidance will always be in accordance with the clear and obvious meaning of Scripture. We believe that what the Bible says God says, and God is not going to contradict in private what he has said in public. For example, the Scriptures indicate that we are to keep our word (Ps. 15:4), so that any voice within suggesting that we break our word or fail to meet a commitment cannot be the voice of God. Similarly, if we feel led to establish a church open only to the rich, we can know that this is not of God. James clearly tells us not to favor the well-to-do (2:1-9).

Second, the voice of God does not prompt us to presumptuous actions. What comes from him will be within the limits of his clear promises. For example, God's Word nowhere says that *all* people who do his will and *only* people who follow him will be materially blessed. Yet we frequently take material affluence as a sign of God's favor, when in fact it may be an indication that we are doing the devil's bidding (Ps. 73:12).

Again, God has never promised students that they will be able to pass their examinations if they do not study; so any suggestion that he will put facts and figures into our minds, simply because we ask him to do so, is misguided.

Third, the guidance of God does not come through fears and apprehensions. "God did not give us a spirit of timidity but a spirit of power and love and self-control" (2 Timothy 1:7). It is not the Spirit of God when we are driven to witness to non-Christians by fear of what other Christians will think of us if we don't; or when we refrain from witnessing through fear of what non-Christians will think of us if we do. It is not the voice of God when we are driven to do anything through fear of other people's tongues or attitudes. It is not the voice of God we are listening to when we hold back from some clear step of faith through fear of not being able to stay on the course.

Fourth, let us remember that the leading of God will usually be confirmed by other Christians. I am not thinking here of a stringent hierarchy of believers where the more mature can determine God's will for less mature disciples. But the New Testament always views the Christian as living in the context of the community of saints (which may be a campus fellowship, a local church, or the like). These brethren are to be consulted as we seek to discern the will of God. If the overwhelming majority of our Christian friends feel that we have misinterpreted the voice of God, we would do well to heed their caution.

Though we must never postpone our response to God once we understand his will, with major decisions it is wise to "sleep on" our impulses. If it is really God who is speaking, his voice will keep sounding with equal insistency tomorrow. God rarely, if ever, shouts. His voice is usually a still, small voice of calm.

God is our Lover, Indweller, Lord, Initiator, Completer and Guide. It is as we live according to our knowledge of who God is that we truly do his will. Next we will see how God's being is revealed in Christ's resurrection and what that means to us as we live the Christian life.

Resurrection and the Life: Dying to Live

7

The resurrection was God's great affirmation that Jesus was who he claimed to be. Paul puts it this way in Romans 1:4, Jesus was "declared with power to be the Son of God by his resurrection from the dead" (NIV).

The Greek word used here and translated "declared" means "to mark something out," "to signify something by marking its limits," "to stake it out as a possession," "to put a seal upon it." By raising Jesus from the dead, God was saying, "This is it; he is the Son of God; this seals it; this proves it."

Peter used this argument when he spoke to the crowds on the day of Pentecost:

*Men of Israel, hear these words: Jesus of Na-
zareth, a man attested to you by God with mighty
works and wonders and signs which God did
through him in your midst, as you yourselves
know—this Jesus, delivered up according to the
definite plan and foreknowledge of God, you
crucified and killed by the hands of lawless men.
But God raised him up, having loosed the pangs
of death, because it was not possible for him to
be held by it. . . . This Jesus God raised up, and
of that we all are witnesses. . . . Let all the house
of Israel therefore know assuredly that God has
made him both Lord and Christ, this Jesus whom
you crucified. (Acts 2:22-24, 32, 36).*

God the Father had made open declarations about
his Son earlier. At the time of his baptism, when
Jesus was about to begin his public ministry, God
spoke from heaven, saying, "This is my beloved
Son" (Matthew 3:17). The miracles that Jesus performed were also an affirmation by God of his
Son.

There is a principle here: God believes in affirming things, in bringing to light hidden things, in un-
veiling veiled things. In fact, he says that there is
nothing hidden that shall not be revealed. Both
good and bad things that are veiled are going to be
unveiled and revealed for what they really are. God
will insist on it.

One is reminded of this principle in the spring.
Hidden things like bulbs reveal themselves. The
hidden life in trees appears in buds. A botanist can
tell one kind of tree from another when their
branches are bare, but to most of us all trees look
alike in winter. When spring brings out their foli-

age, we see each tree in its distinctiveness. This is an illustration of a divine law. There is going to be an authenticating of the true nature and value of everything. That is why you do not need to worry when you see goodness disregarded or even when you see evil covered up. God will see to it that both good and evil become known and declared for what they really are. The resurrection was God's full and final revealing, declaring and authenticating of all Jesus was and did on earth.

Where Is Thy Sting?

But what was it that God was declaring his Son to be by this mighty act? He was declaring Jesus to be the *Conqueror of death*. Raising him from the dead was God's perfect way of making this declaration, the perfect way of affirming it. Nothing less than resurrection would have been appropriate. Nothing else could have adequately declared, affirmed, unveiled who Jesus was, because he was and is, above all, the Conqueror of death. Death is Satan's domain, his kingdom. Causing things to die is his ultimate work. It is the goal and culmination of all he does. Whereas Jesus came that we might have life, Satan comes to bring death. Death to spirit, soul and body is the outcome of Satan's work, even though he disguises it rather skillfully. He is himself the prince of darkness and the lord of death. But Jesus is the Conqueror of death. As Peter said in his sermon on Pentecost, "It was not possible for him to be held by [death]."

Jesus is the Conqueror of death in all its shapes and forms! He is the conqueror of physical death. Therefore, if we are in Christ we can experience power to overcome disease and decay in our bodies even now. Ultimately, we are promised totally new bodies, the culmination of a process already begun on earth (1 Corinthians 15:35-57). We will have a body that no longer decays and deteriorates at all, an imperishable body, like the one that Jesus has now. This is our inheritance if we lay claim to it.

But Jesus is also the breaker of the power of death in every other area of our lives. Death destroys our souls as well as our bodies. It constricts our personalities, our minds and emotions; it restricts, narrows, limits, petrifies. But Jesus has conquered it. Even before God actually raised him from the dead, in the course of his teaching ministry, Jesus had enunciated the truth that he is the resurrection and the life. This is recorded in John 11:25, the story of the raising of Lazarus from the dead.

To read the story of Lazarus and to see in it just a miraculous incident in the life of our Lord is to miss most of the point. To stare with wide-eyed wonder at the fact that Jesus raised a man from the dead, and then to go on to look at the other startling miracles he did is to read John's gospel wrongly.

John records only seven miracles in his gospel. In each case his purpose is far greater than just to let us know that Jesus changed water into wine, healed a child, walked on water, multiplied loaves and fishes. He records the miracles as signs pointing to more significant and eternal realities, realities which we can expect to see happening in our own experience.

"But," you say, "what could be more significant than a man physically dead being restored to life?

It's fantastic! It's incredible! Life and death are the ultimate realities, aren't they? Aren't they the two inescapable facts of human existence, the common denominators that bind us together in fearful unity?"

The Bible's answer is that more dreaded and fearful than physical death is spiritual death, and more glowing and vibrant than physical life is spiritual life. These are the ultimate realities.

Ephesians 2:1 talks about our having been "dead through the trespasses and sins in which [we] once walked." That does not mean lifeless or inert. It means moving in response to the dark spirit of evil, instead of the bright Spirit of God. This is death: awful and unbearable to God, far more real than the cessation of life which we see in a dead human body.

We must ask ourselves: Am I really alive in Christ Jesus? If so, how alive am I? This is the right question to ask, because it is largely due to the anemia of our spiritual lives that spiritual life in general has not been seen for what it is.

Spiritual life is that which combats and overcomes spiritual death. Just as a jet soaring up into the sky roars defiance at the laws of gravity, spiritual life roars defiance at the boastful laws of death. "The law of the Spirit of life in Christ Jesus has set me free from the law of sin and death" (Romans 8:2).

A Present Death

What is spiritual death? Death is that which binds us to an existence governed by selfishness and pride, in which I look out only for what gratifies me and spread my peacock feathers to an admiring world. Death makes me see only my own point of view and fight over little issues that aren't worth a nickel. Death keeps me the slave of self-indulgence, gluttony, lust, roving eyes and uncontrolled desires. Death lulls me into satisfaction with the accomplishment of superficial goals, or fills me with an enervating sense of frustration and worthlessness. Death fills me with fears and anxieties. It makes me worry over yesterday and be anxious about tomorrow. It makes me take out my frustrations on other people and blame them for what is really my fault. It makes me insensitive and dull to what others feel.

Death makes me apathetic to the claims of God, too busy to think about them, too self-satisfied to care. Even if I am allowed to hold the right doctrines and believe that God exists, death will keep me from believing that God is alive and active today. Death keeps me from the knowledge that God is acting today through our prayers (and even without them) to change the hearts of the indifferent, to encourage the fainthearted, and empower the weak.

But life is that which combats death, and Jesus said, "I am the resurrection and the life." He is the embodiment of spiritual life, and when we experience his life within us, banishing death, then we are experiencing a part of the nature of eternity.

Lessons from Lazarus

We earlier mentioned the raising of Lazarus, a story told in John 11:1-44. Jesus' friend Lazarus was taken ill, and his sisters (Mary and Martha) sent for Jesus, hoping he would come and heal him. But by the time he got to Bethany, Lazarus had been dead four days. Both sisters told Jesus, "If you had been here, my brother would not have died" (John 11:21, 32). "Your brother will rise again," Jesus said to Martha (v. 23).

She replied, missing the point, "I know that he will rise again in the resurrection at the last day" (v. 24).

But Jesus responded, "*I* am the resurrection and the life" (v. 25).

Jesus did not say, "I am the *cause* of resurrection, or the *giver* of resurrection, or the *controller* of resurrection." He is those things, too, as he showed when he restored Lazarus to life a little later on. But he wanted to say something more to us than that.

Certainly, Jesus is the One who will be responsible for the ultimate resurrection of our bodies, but he also wants to be new spiritual life in us *now*. There is only one person who can live the Christian life, and that is Jesus Christ.

In John 11, Jesus presents himself as a new life force, a resurrection force that defies the gravitational drag of death.

The life of the age to come—resurrection life— has invaded our age and been implanted in our hearts. There is no reason why you and I should any longer be pitiful slaves of immorality or legalism. We have been offered an original righteousness to overwhelm original sin, a continuous impulse to goodness that can raise us above the patterns of our old nature. God is only waiting for

us to act on the assumption that he is as good as his
Word.

This lesson about the resurrection life is not the
only one to be learned from the story of Lazarus.
Jesus loved Martha, Mary and Lazarus. All he
needed was to "say the word" and Lazarus, like
the centurion's slave (Luke 7:2-10), would have
been healed though Jesus was not present. Instead,
Jesus allowed Lazarus to die, and he even delayed
two extra days so that by the time Jesus arrived in
Bethany Lazarus had been four days in the tomb.
Why did Jesus allow this death? Why did he even
say, "I am glad I was not there" (John 11:15)?

You and I have all sorts of ideas of what we think
is good for us. We think a healthy body, a quiet
mind, a worthwhile job, an ample bank account are
good for us. We think that contentedness, calm,
and a sense of accomplishment are good for us.
These things probably are good. But, if these were
the ultimate good, Jesus, who loved Martha and
Mary and Lazarus well, would have healed Lazarus immediately.

Jesus is not concerned primarily with our contentedness. (That's why, incidentally, I am sometimes worried about contented people—the ones
who are always doing fine. I wonder whether God
hasn't left them.) As I read the Scriptures and as I
observe the experience of men and women in
whose lives God is obviously at work, I see God
taking them up to and beyond what seems to be the
limit of their endurance. Why? It is because, as far
as God is concerned, there's just one ultimate good
for humanity, and that is not contentedness and
peace. The only good is absolute trust in and de-

pendence on him, and this can only be achieved by our being brought time and time again to the end, the real end, of our human resources.

This is why Jesus chose not to heal Lazarus. However desperately ill Lazarus was, provided there was still life, there was still human hope. Jesus had to wait until Lazarus was dead. And when I see people growing in Christ, I often find that they are growing through the experience of death. Jesus is willing to go to great lengths of anguish for us (and for him, for Jesus also wept at Lazarus' death) in order that we will learn the lesson not just of trusting, but of trusting him.

We *should* trust him and love him because it is right to do so, because we have had our eyes opened, because we have caught a glimpse of the glorious truth of who he is and who he is in us. But time and again we do not take God at his Word until we are desperate and all human hope is exhausted. Time and again, we like to try to keep some human expedient in reserve just in case Jesus doesn't come through.

So Jesus, because he loves us, does not hurry to our rescue. He has to make sure that all human hope is finished. God cannot accept a little bit of faith in ourselves and a little bit of faith in him. His plan is death and then life—death to ourselves and then life in him.

Death for Life
Unless you and I are willing to go the whole way with Jesus Christ—the way of death to our cherished ideas of what is good for us and what is due to us—we may never enter into the full experience of

his plan. There will never be the fullness of life in Christ unless we die to our reliance on ourselves. We can never know the creative power of God's life flowing through us until we have yielded to him, surrendered our sovereignty, said a decisive no to unbelief. God's principle is always Good Friday and then Easter Sunday.

For a number of years I was responsible for taking a group of high-school students to visit a nearby nursing home on Sunday afternoons. I would usually go in with them to visit the residents. I found it hard to do. There was a smell permeating the whole place that I did not like, and I had difficulty knowing what to say to these people, some of whom where deaf, some blind, all mentally or physically deteriorated in one way or another. I felt the dehumanizing effects of their illnesses. I felt helpless to console them. I felt repulsed. I wondered if someday I would repulse people.

One afternoon I was particularly tempted to let the students off at the door and tell them I'd be back for them later. I already felt drained and without strength to minister to others. But I looked to the Lord a bit feebly for grace and went in. First we had to see the recreation director who would tell us which residents to visit. She sent all the students off, and I remember hoping that she would say something like: "We really don't have anybody for you to visit this afternoon. Why don't you sit down for a cup of coffee and discuss the program?" But that did not happen. Evidently there was some part of me that needed to die to become completely dependent on Jesus. The director said, "I want you to go into a special wing we have and talk to Mrs.

Randall. She's more senile than the rest and I'm not sure the students could handle her."

Inside I cried out, "Lord, I came in instead of shirking this. What are you doing to me?"

And he was replying, "Yes, but there was rather a lot of Peter Haile in that decision. You're not quite dead yet!"

I thought I was about done for, at that point, and I stumbled into Mrs. Randall's room and started talking to her. As we talked, she drooled from the corner of her mouth. Instead of wiping it with a tissue or handkerchief, she used her hand—not the back of her hand, but the inside of her right hand. The time came for me to leave. and she held out her right hand for me to shake. Finally Lazarus died. At that point I knew the only hope was Jesus. And he came through. I was finally happy, alive to God through Jesus Christ.

I said at the beginning of this chapter that the principle of affirmation runs throughout God's universe; it is a law that he unveils veiled things, brings to light hidden things, speaks unspoken things. We are next to God in all creation. He wants us to do what he has done. He waits for us to affirm by our faith who Jesus is. He wants us, by our acting on the assumption that he is as good as his Word, to show to the world that Jesus is the resurrection and the life.

Bread of Heaven: Table Scraps or Food for Life?

8

Up to this point we have thought of Jesus as the loving Father, Indwelling Spirit, Provider of all we need for life and godliness, Lord, Initiator and Completer, Guide, Resurrection and the Life. Now we will look at Jesus as the Bread of heaven.

Oddly enough, the biblical passage we will use does not even mention the word *bread*. It is my hope, however, that you will soon see its relevance. Paul wrote to the Philippians:

Look out for the dogs, look out for the evil-workers, look out for those who mutilate the flesh. For we are the true circumcision, who worship God in spirit, and glory in Christ Jesus, and put no confidence in the flesh. Though I myself have reason for confidence in the flesh also. If any

*other man thinks he has reason for confidence in
the flesh, I have more: circumcised on the eighth
day, of the people of Israel, of the tribe of Ben-
jamin, a Hebrew born of Hebrews; as to the law,
a Pharisee, as to zeal a persecutor of the church,
as to righteousness under the law blameless. But
whatever gain I had, I counted as loss for the
sake of Christ. Indeed I count everything as loss
because of the surpassing worth of knowing
Christ Jesus my Lord. For his sake I have suf-
fered the loss of all things, and count them as
refuse, in order that I may gain Christ and be
found in him, not having a righteousness of my
own, based on law, but that which is through
faith in Christ, the righteousness from God that
depends on faith; that I may know him and the
power of his resurrection, and may share his suf-
ferings, becoming like him in his death, that if
possible I may attain the resurrection from the
dead. (Phil. 3:2-11)*

This is not the sort of passage you would want to
read before the local pet-owners club. At the very
least, if you read it you would want to reassure the
listeners that domestic pets were not the kind of
dogs Paul was talking about. People of his day did
not keep such pets. He was also probably not talking about the scroungy mutts that may have scav-
enged in the streets of Philippi. He was most likely
using this phrase in a metaphorical sense in verse 2.
He was really telling the Philippians to beware of a
certain group of people.

Specifically, Paul was talking about a group of
people who, surprisingly enough, were highly
moral, but in Paul's view totally unchristian. They

were people who had erected a well-ordered and in many ways most commendable framework of moral and social values. But then they had allowed the very thing that they had been instrumental in creating to become a monster that enslaved them. History has called these people *Judaizers*, and, if I may be permitted the pun, they dogged Paul's footsteps constantly in his proclamation of the gospel. Their name gives us a clue to their problem: they insisted that a full observance of Judaic rites, especially circumcision, was indispensable for acceptance by God.

As we read Philippians 3, it becomes very clear that Paul is attacking not only this particular group of people, but their whole way of life. In other words, the dogs of whom we are to beware are far more numerous than just a small pack of Judaizers. Let's take a look at this issue in more detail.

Crisis of Confidence

The fact of the matter is, and it staggers me to see how many people fail to grasp this, that human beings are dependent beings in every area of life—spiritual, psychological, physical. Every one of us has a basic incompleteness and inadequacy within, which expresses itself in hunger and need and drives us to look for something to satisfy it. As in the physical realm the search may vary in degree, so it does in the psychological realm. One person's psychological needs may be more obvious than another's. But when we say that someone has an inferiority complex, perhaps what we are really communicating is that the person is more conscious of his inadequacy than others. For indeed all of us have inferiority complexes; all of us are inherently insecure, and whether we do it outwardly or not, we are all casting around for whatever we can find to compensate for this feeling.

Paul makes it clear by implication in this Philippians passage that what we do about our hungers, especially our spiritual and psychological hungers, is a crucial question. (Paul was not writing to people who had great physical needs such as for food or shelter.) Spiritual and psychological needs get bound up together in Scripture. Confidence, which is the main topic of this chapter, is a psychological factor, but it is tied right in with our relationship to Jesus Christ.

Now the people Paul calls "dogs" in this passage were people who were meeting this crisis of confidence by looking at themselves and their own accomplishments. They were thankful for their good family background, their adherence to the ceremonial law, their magnificent loyalty to the moral law, and their aggressive campaigning against falsehood and heresy. These things provided them with the confidence to face God and the world. These were the food with which they satisfied their hunger. Paul calls them mangy curs and tells us to beware of them.

The real point Paul is making here is that anything that we rely on other than Christ is refuse, food for dogs. It doesn't have to be good family background or fulfillment of the Law of Moses. These were simply the criteria of success in the particular segment of society Paul was talking to. Paul's dogs are by no means only those who compensate for their insecurity by dwelling on Jewish values. The dogs are, rather, those who base their confidence (for facing God and the world) on meeting the criteria of success of the particular society to which they belong, whatever those criteria may be.

What is some of the dog food that's being fed on in our culture? Suppose a woman feels a sense of insecurity and isolation, but is a relatively good athlete. Chances are that she is going to turn to that athletic ability to compensate for insecurity. If she is thrown in with an unfamiliar group of people and feels insecure, then she will probably do her best to bring the conversation round to athletics. And she will let it be known (subtly or not so subtly) that she is a good track runner or whatever it may be. She will use that accomplishment to get a little security.

Suppose a fellow is not an athlete but a brain. Then whenever he is feeling insecure or put down, he will try to bring the conversation round to grades or College Board scores; he will start talking about Camus or Solzhenitsyn or something.

People who are neither athletes nor scholars will search for something else to feel good about: their looks, their clothes, their family background, their money, their cars, their jokes, their cynicism, their toughness, their way with the opposite sex, their popularity, or even their religion. I know a lot of people who use their religion, their image as good Christians, to compensate for their insecurity.

There is not necessarily anything wrong with being a good athlete, a good scholar, a handsome person, a member of a family of which you can be proud, a fine comedian, a popular date or a good

Christian. The thing that is wrong is trying to use these things as the answer to feelings of inadequacy and inferiority. That's when they become dog food, and people who feed on dog food are dogs.

Poor Miss Nobody

Here's another illustration of the problem. Up until the last few years, single adult women in America have faced a bad situation. They were told that as long as they were single they were nobodies. In those more backward times, a Miss Collins would feel a little insecure and incomplete, because Miss Collinses were intended to become Mrs. Browns or Mrs. Jacksons or Mrs. Somebodies. And in this incomplete state, Miss Collins would constantly be looking around and comparing herself with others. "Am I as pretty as Kathy?" "Am I as witty as Jane?" "Am I as interesting as Elizabeth?"

Finally, Miss Collins would become Mrs. Brown. Thereafter her concern would be no longer with herself and who she was, but with Mr. Brown and who he was. It no longer mattered whether she was as pretty as Miss Banks, as attractive as Miss White or as intelligent as Miss Brimson. What mattered was who Mr. Brown was. She could go to a party and stand beside him, hardly even noticing how she compared with all the other ladies around. She would still dress nicely and talk of interesting things, but now it was done for a different reason— not in order to become Mrs. Brown, but because she was Mrs. Brown. (Dressing nicely is okay if it's a demonstration of who you are. It is dangerous if used as a means to an end.)

Today some of us—men and women alike—still

feel incomplete. We wonder who we are, and what we are, and how we compare to others. But God has a solution for this. Isaiah 54:5 says: "Your Maker is your husband, the LORD of hosts is his name."

Have you and I really found our security in Jesus, or are we still trying to find it in our relationships, accomplishments, and abilities? In other words, are we feeding on the Bread of heaven, richly provided for us in Jesus, or are we nosing around in the dog food to satisfy our hunger?

What the Scriptures say is that Jesus has been made our righteousness. Our right standing with God comes not from what *we* are, but from what *he* is. As I sin and incur guilt before God, I do not have to compensate by my own acts of virtue. That will never work, for "all our righteousnesses are as filthy rags." Instead, I can rely on who Jesus is in the eyes of God to have me fully reinstated. I do not have to grub around and pick up my own droppings, the poisonous scraps of my own accomplishments, to fill my empty belly with, but I can eat the food that really nourishes, food that God himself has prepared for me.

God has said that you and I are so united to Jesus, so merged and fused with him, that his life has become ours. As Paul put it in Galatians 2:20: "I have been crucified with Christ and I no longer live, but Christ lives in me. The life I live in the body, I live by faith in the Son of God, who loved me and gave himself for me" (NIV). In another place, Paul said that it was no longer a matter of having his own righteousness but the righteousness that comes from God through believing in Jesus

(Romans 10:3-4). When the Bible says that Jesus
has been made our righteousness, it means that we
can rely constantly not on ourselves, but on Jesus
who is in us and for us moment by moment.

The question we need to ask ourselves is: To
what extent are we doing this? How are we handling our day-to-day sins? How are we handling
those periodic feelings of alienation from God?
How are we handling the crunch of despair? As our
inner being cries out for a sense of right standing
with God and acceptance with people, do we look
to our own accomplishments and qualifications, or
do we consciously and gratefully accept the fact
that what matters is not who we are but who and
what Jesus is? Do we cast around for accomplishments to cling to and proclaim ourselves saved?

How do I feel when I drive the wrong way up a
one-way street? How do I react when I tip the camp
sailboat over in the middle of the lake? What do I
do when I call somebody by the wrong name? How
do I react when I have failed spiritually, when sin
has encroached, when my witness has been ineffec-
tive, when others have won the spiritual honors,
when my nice little theological system has toppled?
If an experience like that has thrown me—and
which of us can say it never does—then the message is clear: I was trusting in myself and my own
spirituality, not in God who raises the dead.

What about failure with our peers? When you
and I have fallen short of the standards, what has it
done to us? How have we reacted? If it has thrown
us into depression and gloom, then we can know
beyond a shadow of a doubt that our previous confidence lay chiefly in feeling, with little Jack

Horner, "What a good boy am I!" It was a confidence based on our success in attaining acceptance. It was not an abject dependence on Jesus.

What is my reaction to professional failure? Have I been shown to be the puppet of success, carried along only by self-esteem and the plaudits of the crowd? I am afraid I have, time and again.

Spiritual attainment, moral integrity and professional skill are all good things. It is only when we find in these things the source of our confidence toward God and humanity that we fall into the category that Paul condemns so vigorously.

Of course, all this is not to say that instead of taking pride in our attainments, we should start taking pride in our failures. The idea is not to start substituting negative criteria for positive ones. This is what the hippies did in the 1960s. They developed a cult of failure and unorthodoxy and became proud of themselves for doing it. But if that's what we do as Christians, we have fallen into the same pit. We are resting our faith in ourselves, in our failures.

The Final Test

Throughout all I have said, I have repeatedly spoken of our confidence toward God and humanity. I have done this deliberately, because I believe that just as the real test of our love for God comes in our relationship to people (see 1 John 4:20), so the real test of our reliance on the integrity and love of God comes in our relationship to others. Do we require a righteousness of our own (and compare ourselves with others) or not? This is the test.

Paul's passionate cry was: "God forbid that I

should glory, save in the cross of our Lord Jesus
Christ, by whom the world is crucified unto me,
and I unto the world" (Galatians 6:14 KJV). The
cross was the act whereby God put Jesus in our
place and said that we could live by who he is instead of by who we are. And Paul wanted to line up
with God instead of with the world.

In his humanity, Jesus himself had to face this
same problem, when Satan tempted him saying, "If
you are the Son of God, command this stone to become bread" (Luke 4:3). Note how Satan started
with *if*. He tempted Jesus to doubt what he knew to
be true about himself. At the same time, Satan was
tempting him to doubt the sufficiency and the timing of God's provision: "Take the initiative into
your own hands. God has forgotten or he is late.
You won't get any bread from him." This is the way
it came to Jesus and this is the way it will come to
us. The temptation will question what God has
done in our lives in making us his own redeemed
children and question the sufficiency and the timing
of his provision of grace. We will be tempted to act
as though these were inadequate. We will be told to
provide food of our own—dog food.

If an honest analysis of where our confidence
lies shows us to be trusting in our own righteousness, let us not despair. God is waiting and longing
to work on this problem with us. In fact, most of
God's dealings with us throughout our lives are a
concerted and calculated effort to get us to transfer
the whole basis of our confidence from ourselves to
him, to turn from dog food to the bread of heaven.

The Kingdom Restored

9

C. S. Lewis's fantasy *The Lion, the Witch and the Wardrobe* is one of my favorite books. In this children's story, four youngsters from England find themselves magically admitted to the land of Narnia. Narnia is a fascinating place where animals, such as fauns and beavers, talk and make plans just like·people. Narnia was created by Aslan, the great and powerful lion. But when the children arrive, Narnia is under the influence of a wicked White Witch.

One of the children, Edmund, turns traitor and joins forces with the Witch. In order to save Edmund's life, Aslan gives himself to be killed in Edmund's place. On a great Stone Table he is bound and slaughtered.

The next day two of the other children, Susan and Lucy, look in disbelief at the empty Table and Aslan, alive and strong.

"But what does it all mean?" asks Susan, finally satisfied that Aslan is not a ghost.

"It means," Aslan explains, "that though the Witch knew the Deep Magic, there is a magic deeper still which she did not know. . . . If she could have looked a little further back, . . . she would have known that when a willing victim who had committed no treachery was killed in a traitor's stead, the Table would crack and Death itself would start working backwards."

Reversing the Trends of Life

Death itself would start working backwards! That is what Christianity is all about. The death and resurrection of Jesus Christ has set in motion a process that runs counter to all that is going on around us. The whole of created life is ruled by a law of depreciation. It is in the nature of things to disorganize, to deteriorate, to go from good to bad. We see it in every area of life. How much do we spend each year simply repairing what has broken? How much do we get when we take our eight-year-old car back to the dealer where we got it and ask for a refund?

Even people depreciate. We scale the middle years of life and find our limbs won't do what they used to do; our children can beat us in a race. We spend hours cleaning the house and two days later we have to start all over again. Things don't get cleaner; they get dirtier.

Strength ebbs in this world. As the prophet Isaiah put it, "Even youths shall faint and be weary, and young men shall fall exhausted" (40:30).

But something happened when Jesus Christ died and rose again. The gravitational flow was reversed. Death started working backwards. The Bible calls it the coming of the kingdom of God. In the kingdom of God things work the other way around. Wrong gets turned to right; night to day; the weary become stronger; and the longer we live the younger we get. What is perishable does not go bad. It gets steadily more full of life until it is finally clothed with immortality. That is the kingdom of God.

How would you describe the kingdom of God? There seem to be few concepts so prominent in the Bible that have so largely eluded our grasp.

One of the chief problems, I think, is that we tend to think of a kingdom as an area, a territory, ruled by a king. This definition may fit with the doctrine of the millennial rule of Christ on Earth. But it does not fit with other biblical references which speak of the kingdom of God as a part of our present experience, something that is entered into here and now. Nor is it congruent with the message of the "parables of the kingdom," all of which seem to suggest a principle of life rather than an area or territory. "The kingdom of heaven is like treasure hidden in a field . . ." (Matthew 13:44). "The kingdom of heaven is like a net which was thrown into the sea . . ." (Matthew 13:47). "The kingdom of heaven may be compared to a king who gave a marriage feast for his son . . ." (Matthew 22:2). The New Testament even presents the kingdom not as something that we enter into, but as something that enters into us. Luke 17:21 says,

"The kingdom of God is within you" (NIV).

The most helpful solution to this problem that I have come across is the suggestion that the word *kingdom* here means not an area or territory, but the reign or sovereignty of the ruler. This interpretation is beautifully illustrated in Psalm 145:11: "They shall speak of the glory of thy kingdom, and tell of thy power." To speak of the glory of his kingdom is to tell of his power. His kingdom is his sovereignty in action.

During World War 2, Holland was occupied by Germans. But Queen Wilhelmina still had her kingdom. Her reign essentially continued because the people of Holland were still loyal to her and only her. This is the kind of sovereignty—a rule in the hearts and lives of people—that is expressed in the phrase *the kingdom of God*.

When Jesus said that we must receive the kingdom of God as little children, he meant that child-like submission is necessary before God can rule our hearts. The whole thing must be thought of in terms of relationships, not geography. It is a question of where the power and authority reside. When we are told to "seek first the kingdom of God," the object of our quest is not heaven or the organizational church. It is God's rule in our hearts and lives.

When we pray, "Thy kingdom come," we are not praying for heaven to come to earth. We are praying for his will to be done on earth as it is in heaven. Our petition is for God to reign, to manifest his kingship and power, to put to flight every enemy of righteousness and establish his divine rule.

It is the kingdom of God in this sense that the gospel is all about. This is what Jesus came to inaugurate. He came proclaiming the good news of the kingdom; namely, the news that the kingship of God can now reside in the hearts of men and women through the new birth. The life of the kingdom of God, life with God at its center, the source and substance of its motivation, is available to people even as they live in this present evil world. A loyalty to God, deeply subversive to the present regime, can be planted in people's hearts, setting up pockets of resistance throughout enemy-occupied territory.

Evidence from the Early Church

The more I read the New Testament, the more impressed I am with the fact that the early Christians clearly understood this sense of the kingdom. It made them intensely "otherworldly" (in the *good* sense of that term). They took every opportunity to cut themselves loose form the strings of this world and hazarded their all on the reality of the kingdom of God. There was a youthful irresponsibility, almost a total lack of caution. New believers sold their houses and lands. They let go of the symbols of their old lives and committed all to heavenly citizenship.

Why was this? How do we account for this attitude in people who by and large were less inclined to switch loyalties and allegiances than we are? One reason was the nature of the preaching. The thrust of apostolic preaching was that God was offering to people in this world the chance to enter a totally new dimension of life. God was giving people the opportunity here and now of crossing the boundary separating this age from the age to come. According to the apostolic preaching, God was holding out the chance of becoming a totally new kind of person: not a Jew nor a Gentile, but a creature of the age to come, a being possessed of the life of the eternal God himself. According to Peter, Paul, and the rest of the apostles, that whole realm over which Jesus Christ reigns supreme had broken in upon this world. And the new believers were being invited to join it by faith. All this was what Jesus had been talking about earlier: "The kingdom of heaven" was at hand, he said. And now, through the portals of his death and resurrection, it had come.

This was the gospel that came to the early Christians. They were told that through the death and resurrection of Jesus Christ the reign of God's Messiah had begun. They could join this new kingdom if they would act on the assumption that God was as good as his Word. It was an intensely otherworldly message. They were being offered the chance of being caught up in something infinitely bigger than themselves, an invasion from another world which gave them the chance of becoming other-worldlings.

.This is the primary reason why the early Christians were so gloriously free from the earthliness that seems to grip us so strongly. The second reason, I believe, was that they were far more deeply convinced than we are that this present world is evil and temporary.

We often fail to see the gospel for what it really is. We do not have the cosmic view of Christianity which so characterized apostolic preaching. Christianity has been presented to us either as an oversimplified plan of salvation or as a good alternative to psychotherapy. It has been humanized almost beyond recognition. The incredible fact that the great Creator God is offering to us eternal union with himself through his Son Jesus Christ has been watered down to a presentation of certain theological propositions and psychological formulas. And no person in his right senses is going to cut ties to this world for anything so insignificant as that.

Unlike the early Christians, we also do not recognize this present world as evil and temporary. Of course, we deplore the little evils that get in our way, like being cheated, having to pay taxes, having to compete to get into medical school, having difficulty getting a job, and so on. Sometimes we even contemplate the really big evils, like world hunger and the atomic bomb. But we fail to recognize the fundamental spirit of this age. We forget that the state of the world provoked God to declare war and invade. We do not distinguish in the spirit of this age the very face of Satan. How can we say we have seen the truth about the world when most of us who call ourselves Christians embrace rather than repudiate it? We may make academic stands against worldliness, but we need a little more underground activity on the part of the subjects of the King. How many of the usurper's bridges have we blown up recently? Do we hate his propaganda enough to have started putting out an underground newspaper of our own? He doesn't distribute the wealth of the world very equitably; have we done anything about it?

Not all of us, of course, are called to be freedom fighters with the underground. Though we are all on the same team, some of us are called to be ambassadors.

Singing the Lord's Song in a Strange Land

An ambassador is a foreigner in the country where he is living. He is an outsider, and he must accept that fact and remember it all the time. His real home is in another country, where he was born and raised. His ultimate allegiance and loyalty are not to the country where he is living, but to the one from which he came. While he is living in the foreign country, he will be law-abiding, so long as those laws do not conflict with his role as ambassador.

The ambassador rarely finds himself completely at ease. He has a different cultural background and set of values. In his thinking he tends to start from different premises than the locals and comes out with different conclusions. His ultimate goals are different.

An ambassador feels out-of-it because he has no real investments where he lives. He is only a temporary resident. He won't be staying any longer than the term of service for which he was sent. He is not interested in sinking roots.

An ambassador sees discrepancies between his qualifications and those the people expect. They seem to think that different things are important, and he is faced with the problem of having to reconcile himself to not meeting those qualifications. He has to be satisfied with the reassurance that his king thinks he has what it takes. It is sometimes hard for him not to look for rewards and honors from the people he lives with. But, when he's in his right mind, he knows that what really matters is to earn the honor of his own country.

An ambassador is a representative. He doesn't go to the foreign country for his own sake, or for a vacation or to visit relatives. He goes because he is sent—to be the representative of his king. He is not there to air his own views, or propound his own theories about international relations or economic policy. The ambassador's task is to represent his government's plans and policies. He is there to represent the patterns of behavior in his own country, the way the people think, their attitudes toward economic affairs, their standards of living, their customs, their approach to art and letters and music, their concepts of the origin of the universe and the meaning of life.

Most of the people in the foreign country where he is living will never have a chance to see his sovereign in person. Therefore, the ambassador has to represent him wherever he goes. The idea is that when the people of the foreign country have seen the ambassador it should be as though they had seen the king. There is a very real sense in which they are going to judge his king by him.

An ambassador lives in an embassy. He needs a home away from home where he lives and has his headquarters. So he gathers around him a little group of his countrymen, people owing allegiance to his sovereign and his government, loyal and true to his homeland, who speak his language, eat the same food he eats, hold to the same standards, think the same way, have been raised in the same culture, have submitted to the same authority. These people establish a little island of their own in this foreign land, and in it they enjoy each other's company and talk freely about home and kindred.

In the embassy, the staff receive messages from their home government: directives about policy, instructions about the attitudes they should adopt toward particular people and theories. In the embassy, they are free to talk over these instructions and see whether they understand them properly. They work out courses of action to implement policies. In the embassy, they can discuss the situation around them, and from the embassy they can send messages back home reporting what is happening. Here, as nowhere else, the ambassador can share his problems and look for help and advice and guidance from his fellow citizens.

Finally, *an ambassador helps those who wish to emigrate* to his country. He must make clear what the requirements are, how they go about applying for immigration rights. Then he must encourage people to emigrate, and pass on to them his sovereign's warm and earnest invitation.

We are all ambassadors for Christ, representing our Lord in a foreign land. He is the loving Father who waits for us freely to turn to him. He is the Indwelling Spirit who provides all the power that we need for godliness. Jesus is our Lord, and Lord of all that happens in our lives and in the world. He is the Initiator and Completer, the One who carries out his will through us. He is our Guide. Jesus is the Resurrection and the Life, who makes even death work backwards to life. He is the Bread of heaven, who gives us the identity we need for security in this world.

Having faith in God means acting on these things; it means being who we already are in Christ.